THE GRAND FINALE

A well planned goodbye

A Comprehensive
End-of-Life Planner & Journal

Published by:
SkillBinder Press
c/o Epoxy Dogs LLC
5698 Lamplighter Dr.
Girard, Ohio, USA 44420

www.skillbinder.com

Print ISBN: 979-8-218-86182-7

Printed in the United States of America

First Edition – 2025

This book was produced using independent publishing tools and is distributed through Lulu.com
Visit www.lulu.com for more information.

9 798218 861827

THE GRAND FINALE
A Well-Planned Goodbye

A COMPREHENSIVE
END-OF-LIFE PLANNER AND JOURNAL

2025 EDITION

Authored by: _____

Signature: _____

Dated: _____

HOW TO USE THIS PLANNER – 2025 EDITION

Planning for the future—especially when it comes to the end of life—is one of the most meaningful gifts you can give to your loved ones. It may not be an easy task, but once completed, this planner will serve as a guiding light, easing the burden on those left behind and ensuring your wishes are honored.

This thoughtfully designed End-of-Life Planner provides a clear and compassionate framework for organizing the essential details your loved ones may need. It is more than just a document—it's a way to leave behind clarity, comfort, and guidance during a difficult time.

Scan the QR code with your phone.

Inside, you will have space to record:

- Personal and medical details for easy reference.
- Information about your dependents and pets to ensure they are cared for.
- A complete financial overview, including bank accounts, loans, and investments.
- A contact list of those to notify in case of your passing.
- Insurance policies and beneficiaries to simplify next steps.
- An inventory of personal belongings, from real estate to treasured keepsakes.
- A checklist of accounts and memberships that need attention.
- Personal reflections and final wishes, ensuring your voice is heard even in your absence.

Guidance at Every Step

To make this process even easier, each chapter includes a QR code that you can scan with your phone to access helpful tips. These resources will provide insights, suggestions, and encouragement as you work through each section, ensuring you get the most out of this planner.

We understand that everyone's journey is unique, which is why this planner is designed to be flexible. Some sections may not apply to you—fill out what matters most, and revisit when needed. Additional blank pages are included for anything personal you'd like to share.

A Note of Encouragement

This planner is not just about logistics; it's about love, legacy, and peace of mind. By taking the time to organize these details now, you are offering an incredible act of kindness to those who will carry on your story.

Please note: This document is not legally binding and does not replace a will or other legal estate planning documents. To avoid confusion, ensure the information here aligns with your official paperwork.

Thank you for trusting The Grand Finale: A Well-Planned Goodbye to be part of your journey. Your thoughtful planning today will bring immeasurable comfort and clarity to those you love tomorrow.

TABLE OF CONTENTS

Additional Notes:

SECTION 1
PERSONAL INFORMATION
(QUICK REFERENCE SECTION)
More detailed options available in later sections

START HERE, AND START STRONG—YOUR FULL LEGAL NAME, IDENTIFIERS, AND CITIZENSHIP STATUS ARE ESSENTIAL FOR EVERYTHING FROM LEGAL DOCUMENTS TO FINAL ARRANGEMENTS.

Scan the QR code
with your phone.

PERSONAL INFORMATION (QUICK REFERENCE SECTION) – 2025 EDITION

Gender Pronouns:

☐ He/Him/His ☐ She/Her/Hers ☐ They/Them/Theirs

☐ Ze/Hir/Hirs ☐ Ey/Em/Eir ☐ Other: _____

Legal & Biographical Information:

Full Name: _____

Full Name At Birth (if applicable): _____

Date of Birth: _____ Place of Birth (City, Country): _____

Born Abroad or U.S. Territory? ☐ Yes ☐ No   If yes, specify: _____

Social Security Number (SSN): _____

Identification & Citizenship:

U.S. Driver's License Number: _____

State or Territory of Issuance: _____ Expiration Date: _____

Passport(s):

Passport Number: _____ Country of Issuance: _____

Passport Number (if applicable): _____ Country of Issuance: _____

Dual or Multiple Citizenship? ☐ Yes ☐ No   If yes, list countries: _____

PERSONAL INFORMATION (QUICK REFERENCE SECTION) – 2025 EDITION

Current & Past Addresses:

Present Address: _____

City: _____ State/Territory: _____ Zipcode: _____

Country (if residing abroad): _____

Past Address: _____

City: _____ State/Territory: _____ Zipcode: _____

Country (if residing abroad): _____

Present Address: _____

City: _____ State/Territory: _____ Zipcode: _____

Country (if residing abroad): _____

Present Address: _____

City: _____ State/Territory: _____ Zipcode: _____

Country (if residing abroad): _____

Phone Number(s):

1. _____   2. _____

3. _____   4. _____

Emergency Contacts:

1.   Name: _____ Relationship: _____ Phone: _____

2.   Name: _____ Relationship: _____ Phone: _____

3.   Name: _____ Relationship: _____ Phone: _____

4.   Name: _____ Relationship: _____ Phone: _____

5.   Name: _____ Relationship: _____ Phone: _____

PERSONAL INFORMATION (QUICK REFERENCE SECTION) – 2025 EDITION

Family Information:

Father's Full Name: _____

Mother's Full Name: _____

Stepfather's Full Name (If applicable): _____

Stepmother's Full Name (If applicable): _____

Relationship Status:

☐ Single   ☐ Divorced   ☐ Widowed   ☐ Common Law

Spouse/Significant Other's Full Name (If applicable): _____

Spouse/Significant Other's Contact Info (If applicable): _____

Children('s) / Dependent('s) Information (Full Name / Gender / Age):

1. Name: _____ Gender: ☐ Male ☐ Female ☐ Other Age: _____

2. Name: _____ Gender: ☐ Male ☐ Female ☐ Other Age: _____

3. Name: _____ Gender: ☐ Male ☐ Female ☐ Other Age: _____

4. Name: _____ Gender: ☐ Male ☐ Female ☐ Other Age: _____

5. Name: _____ Gender: ☐ Male ☐ Female ☐ Other Age: _____

6. Name: _____ Gender: ☐ Male ☐ Female ☐ Other Age: _____

7. Name: _____ Gender: ☐ Male ☐ Female ☐ Other Age: _____

8. Name: _____ Gender: ☐ Male ☐ Female ☐ Other Age: _____

Other Family Members: _____

PERSONAL INFORMATION (QUICK REFERENCE SECTION) – 2025 EDITION

Religious & Spiritual Preferences:

Religious Affiliation / Faith Tradition: _____

Place of Worship (Name and Address): _____

_____

Clergy / Spiritual Leader Name & Contact:

Name: _____   Phone: _____

Email: _____

End-of-Life Religious Preferences:

Last Rites: ☐Yes ☐No ☐Undecided

Clergy Present: ☐Yes ☐No ☐Undecided

Scripture Preferences: _____

Prayer Style: _____

Burial Riturals: _____

Work and Career Info:

Employment Status: ☐Employed ☐Unemployed ☐Self Employed

☐Entrepreneur ☐Retired

Employer's Name (if applicable): _____

Employer's Address: _____

Employer's Phone: _____

Supervisor / Contact Person: _____

Notes: _____

PERSONAL INFORMATION (QUICK REFERENCE SECTION) – 2025 EDITION

Security & Digital Access:

Location of Will / Legal Documents: _____

Phone Unlock Code: _____

Password Manager Info: _____

Backup Code Location / Master Password Holder: _____

Key Online Accounts (use Section 7 to add more details): _____

Digital Document Locations: _____

Location of Critical Documents & Keys:

Passport / ID: _____

Birth Certificate: _____

Marriage / Divorce / Domestic Partnership Certificates: _____

Social Security Card: _____

Driver's License / State ID: _____

Insurance Policies: _____

Real Estate Titles / Deeds: _____

Safe Deposit Box Info: _____

Storage / Locker / PO Box Keys: _____

Home / Car / Office Keys: _____

Other: _____

PERSONAL INFORMATION (QUICK REFERENCE SECTION) – 2025 EDITION

Additional Notes:

(Message to Family / Loved Ones / Special Instructions)

Additional Notes:

SECTION 2
MEDICAL INFORMATION

DON'T ASSUME OTHERS KNOW YOUR MEDICAL HISTORY—DOCUMENT IT CLEARLY TO AVOID CONFUSION OR DELAYS IN CARE WHEN TIME MATTERS MOST

Scan the QR code
with your phone.

MEDICAL INFORMATION – 2025 EDITION

Physician's Infomation:

1. Primary Doctor's Full Name: _____

   Doctor's Specialty: _____

   Clinic / Hospital Name: _____

   Doctor's Phone Number: _____

   Doctor's Email (if known): _____

   Emergency Contact at Clinic: _____

2. Doctor's Full Name: _____

   Doctor's Specialty: _____

   Clinic / Hospital Name: _____

   Doctor's Phone Number: _____

   Doctor's Email (if known): _____

   Emergency Contact at Clinic: _____

3. Doctor's Full Name: _____

   Doctor's Specialty: _____

   Clinic / Hospital Name: _____

   Doctor's Phone Number: _____

   Doctor's Email (if known): _____

   Emergency Contact at Clinic: _____

Health Insurance & ID Details:

   Notes: _____

MEDICAL INFORMATION – 2025 EDITION

Medications:

Current Prescription Medications (Include medication name, dosage, frequency, and reason.):

MEDICATION NAME	DOSAGE	FREQUENCY	REASON

Over-the-Counter Medications/Supplements (Include brand name and purpose):

MEDICAL INFORMATION – 2025 EDITION

Pharmacy Name & Location: _____

Pharmacy Phone Number: _____

Allergies & Reactions:

Known Allergies (Medications, Foods, Environmental): _____

_____

_____

Allergic Reactions & Treatment: _____

_____

_____

Medical Conditions & History:

Chronic Illnesses / Diagnosed Conditions: _____

_____

_____

Surgeries & Major Procedures (with dates): _____

_____

_____

Significant Past Hospitalizations (with dates & reasons): _____

_____

_____

_____

_____

MEDICAL INFORMATION – 2025 EDITION

Organ Donation & Advance Directives:

Organ Donor? ☐ Yes ☐ No

☐ Registered with State/Donor Network (Specify): _____

Location of Organ Donor Card or Registration Info: _____

Living Will Completed? ☐ Yes ☐ No

     Date Created: _____ Location of Document: _____

Do Not Resuscitate (DNR) in Place? ☐ Yes ☐ No

     Date Created: _____ Location of Document: _____

Healthcare Proxy / Power of Attorney:

Name of Healthcare POA: _____

Relationship to You: _____

Phone Number: _____ Email: _____

POA Document Location: _____

Insurance & Coverage Details:

Health Insurance Provider Name: _____

Plan Number / Group Number: _____

Policy Holder Name (if different): _____

Insurance Contact Phone: _____

Secondary / Supplemental Insurance (if applicable): _____

_____

_____

_____

MEDICAL INFORMATION – 2025 EDITION

Healthcare Facilities:

Closest Emergency Room (ER): _____

Preferred Hospital for an Emergency: _____

Additional Notes or Special Instructions (Example: Religious restrictions on care, people in attendance, etc.):

LEGAL AND ESTATE PLANNING

LEGAL CLARITY EQUALS PEACE OF MIND—BE SPECIFIC AND ENSURE YOUR WILL, EXECUTOR, AND LEGAL CONTACTS ARE CLEARLY NAMED AND EASY TO LOCATE.

Scan the QR code
with your phone.

LEGAL AND ESTATE PLANNING – 2025 EDITION

Will & Estate Overview:

Do you have a Last Will & Testament? ☐ Yes ☐ No ☐ In Progress

Date Last Updated: _____

Location of Original Document: _____

Other Estate Documents (e.g., Trusts, Codicils): _____

_____

_____

_____

Lawyer Information:

1.   Lawyer's Name: _____

      Address: _____

2.   Lawyer's Name: _____

      Address: _____

3.   Lawyer's Name: _____

      Address: _____

Legal and Financial Contacts:

Estate Attorney:

      Full Name: _____   Phone Number: _____

      Firm: _____   Email: _____

Financial Advisor / Estate Planner:

      Full Name: _____   Phone Number: _____

      Company: _____   Email: _____

LEGAL AND ESTATE PLANNING – 2025 EDITION

Executor Details:

Full Name: _____

Relationship to You: _____

Phone Number: _____ Email Address: _____

Mailing Address: _____

Is the Executor Aware? ☐ Yes ☐ No

Has the Executor Accepted the Role? ☐ Yes ☐ No

Alternate Executor(s) Details:

1. Full Name: _____ Phone Number: _____

    Email: _____ Relationship: _____

2. Full Name: _____ Phone Number: _____

    Email: _____ Relationship: _____

Additional Notes:

Document Stating Executor Role Is Located At: _____

Executor Compensation Preference:

☐ Waive   ☐ Flate Fee $_____   ☐ Hourly $_____   ☐ As Allowed by Law

Special Notes or Instructions for Executor: _____

_____

_____

_____

_____

_____

LEGAL AND ESTATE PLANNING – 2025 EDITION

Power of Attorney (POA):

Financial POA

    Agent Name: _____

    Contact Info: _____

    Relationship: _____

    Effective When: ☐ Immediately   ☐ Upon Incapacity

Healthcare Proxy (cross-reference Section 2)

    Proxy Name: _____

    Alternate Proxy: _____

Other POAs / Legal Agents

    Role & Name: _____

    Notes or Limitations: _____

Supporting Legal Documents:

Guardianship Designation (for minor/dependent):

    Guardian(s): _____

    Document Location: _____

Burial or Cremation Authorization: ☐ Burial ☐ Cremation

    Signed Form Location: _____

HIPAA Release Form Location: _____

Digital or Social Media Will Exists (More details provided in section 7)? ☐ Yes ☐ No

    Executor or Digital Manager Name: _____

    Location of Document / Passwords: _____

LEGAL AND ESTATE PLANNING – 2025 EDITION

Personal Safe Details:

Type & Brand of Safe: _____

Location: _____

Access Code or Key Location: _____

Individuals with Access: _____

Content Overview (Will, passports, deeds, etc.): _____

Instructions for Opening / Access: _____

Safe Deposit Box:

Bank Name & Branch Location: _____

Box Number: _____

Who Has the Key?: _____

Contents (High-level Overview): _____

Notes:

_____

_____

_____

_____

_____

_____

_____

_____

_____

Additional Notes:

SECTION 4
FINANCE & BUSINESS

LEAVE NO ACCOUNT BEHIND—GATHER DETAILS ON EVERYTHING FROM
BANK ACCOUNTS TO CAR PAYMENTS TO GIVE YOUR LOVED
ONES A CLEAR FINANCIAL ROADMAP.

SkillBinder

Scan the QR code
with your phone.

Bank Accounts & Balances:

1.   Bank Name(s): _____

    Approx. Balances: _____

    Account Locations (Paper or Digital): _____

2.   Bank Name(s): _____

    Approx. Balances: _____

    Account Locations (Paper or Digital): _____

3.   Bank Name(s): _____

    Approx. Balances: _____

    Account Locations (Paper or Digital): _____

4.   Bank Name(s): _____

    Approx. Balances: _____

    Account Locations (Paper or Digital): _____

5.   Bank Name(s): _____

    Approx. Balances: _____

    Account Locations (Paper or Digital): _____

6.   Bank Name(s): _____

    Approx. Balances: _____

    Account Locations (Paper or Digital): _____

7.   Bank Name(s): _____

    Approx. Balances: _____

    Account Locations (Paper or Digital): _____

8.   Bank Name(s): _____

    Approx. Balances: _____

    Account Locations (Paper or Digital): _____

Cash on Hand:

Amount: $ _____

Location(s): _____

Investments & Brokerages:

1. Firm Name: _____

    Account Info / Broker Contact: _____

    Document Location: _____

2. Firm Name: _____

    Account Info / Broker Contact: _____

    Document Location: _____

3. Firm Name: _____

    Account Info / Broker Contact: _____

    Document Location: _____

4. Firm Name: _____

    Account Info / Broker Contact: _____

    Document Location: _____

Retirement Plans & Pensions:

Plan Type(s): _____

Provider(s): _____

Location of Plan Documents: _____

FINANCE & BUSINESS – 2025 EDITION

Cryptocurrencies & Precious Metals:

Wallet Location / Access Info: _____

Precious Metal Location(s): _____

Income Sources (Rental, pension, annuity, etc.):

1. Type of Income: _____

   Contact Info / Payment Details: _____

2. Type of Income: _____

   Contact Info / Payment Details: _____

3. Type of Income: _____

   Contact Info / Payment Details: _____

4. Type of Income: _____

   Contact Info / Payment Details: _____

Debts, Mortgages & Liabilities:

Creditor Name(s): _____

Outstanding Balance(s): _____

Payment Due Dates: _____

Business Vehicles & Leases (i.e. Fleet vehicles):

1. Make/Model: _____

   Title / Lease Location: _____

2. Make/Model: _____

   Title / Lease Location: _____

3. Make/Model: _____

   Title / Lease Location: _____

4.   Make/Model: _____

       Title / Lease Location: _____

5.   Make/Model: _____

       Title / Lease Location: _____

6.   Make/Model: _____

       Title / Lease Location: _____

7.   Make/Model: _____

       Title / Lease Location: _____

8.   Make/Model: _____

       Title / Lease Location: _____

9.   Make/Model: _____

       Title / Lease Location: _____

10. Make/Model: _____

       Title / Lease Location: _____

Business Real Estate Properties:

1.   Address: _____

       Mortgage Info / Deed Location: _____

2.   Address: _____

       Mortgage Info / Deed Location: _____

3.   Address: _____

       Mortgage Info / Deed Location: _____

4.   Address: _____

       Mortgage Info / Deed Location: _____

5.   Address: _____

      Mortgage Info / Deed Location: _____

6.   Address: _____

      Mortgage Info / Deed Location: _____

7.   Address: _____

      Mortgage Info / Deed Location: _____

8.   Address: _____

      Mortgage Info / Deed Location: _____

9.   Address: _____

      Mortgage Info / Deed Location: _____

10.   Address: _____

      Mortgage Info / Deed Location: _____

Business Ownership:

1.   Business Name: _____

      Type of Ownership (Sole Proprietorship, Partnership, Corporation, LLC): _____

      Successor or Sale Plan: _____

2.   Business Name: _____

      Type of Ownership (Sole Proprietorship, Partnership, Corporation, LLC): _____

      Successor or Sale Plan: _____

3.   Business Name: _____

      Type of Ownership (Sole Proprietorship, Partnership, Corporation, LLC): _____

      Successor or Sale Plan: _____

4.   Business Name: _____

   Type of Ownership (Sole Proprietorship, Partnership, Corporation, LLC): _____

   Successor or Sale Plan: _____

5.   Business Name: _____

   Type of Ownership (Sole Proprietorship, Partnership, Corporation, LLC): _____

   Successor or Sale Plan: _____

6.   Business Name: _____

   Type of Ownership (Sole Proprietorship, Partnership, Corporation, LLC): _____

   Successor or Sale Plan: _____

7.   Business Name: _____

   Type of Ownership (Sole Proprietorship, Partnership, Corporation, LLC): _____

   Successor or Salc Plan: _____

8.   Business Name: _____

   Type of Ownership (Sole Proprietorship, Partnership, Corporation, LLC): _____

   Successor or Sale Plan: _____

Financial Advisor Contact:

   Name: _____

   Phone / Email: _____

Access to Statements:

   Paper or Digital? ☐ Paper   ☐ Digital

   Stored At / Password Info: _____

Additional Notes:

SECTION 5
BENEFICIARIES & INHERITANCE

BE CLEAR AND SPECIFIC—NAMING YOUR BENEFICIARIES AND WHAT THEY ARE TO RECEIVE AVOIDS CONFUSION, PREVENTS DISPUTES, AND ENSURES YOUR INTENTIONS ARE HONORED EXACTLY AS YOU IMAGINED.

Scan the QR code
with your phone.

Life and Health Insurance Policies:

1. Company Name: _____

   Policy Type: _____

   Account Number: _____

   Contacts: _____

   Amount: _____

   Beneficiary: _____

   Notes: _____

2. Company Name: _____

   Policy Type: _____

   Account Number: _____

   Contacts: _____

   Amount: _____

   Beneficiary: _____

   Notes: _____

3. Company Name: _____

   Policy Type: _____

   Account Number: _____

   Contacts: _____

   Amount: _____

   Beneficiary: _____

   Notes: _____

Employee Benefits:

Who is/are the Beneficiary(ies)?: _____

Account Number: _____

Contacts: _____

Notes: _____

Social Security:

Who is/are the Beneficiary(ies)?: _____

Account Number: _____

Contacts: _____

Notes: _____

Retirement:

Who is/are the Beneficiary(ies)?: _____

Account Number: _____

Contacts: _____

Notes: _____

Veteran's Benefits:

Who is/are the Beneficiary(ies)?: _____

Account Number: _____

Contacts: _____

Notes: _____

BENEFICIARIES & INHERITANCE – 2025 EDITION

Primary & Contingent Beneficiaries:

Primary Name(s): _____

Contingent Name(s): _____

Assigned Beneficiaries on Accounts:

Account Type / Beneficiary Name(s): _____

Location of Confirmation Docs: _____

Specific Bequests (Heirlooms, Gifts):

1.   Item: _____ Recipient Name(s): _____

      Bequest List Location: _____

2.   Item: _____ Recipient Name(s): _____

      Bequest List Location: _____

3.   Item: _____ Recipient Name(s): _____

      Bequest List Location: _____

4.   Item: _____ Recipient Name(s): _____

      Bequest List Location: _____

5.   Item: _____ Recipient Name(s): _____

      Bequest List Location: _____

6.   Item: _____ Recipient Name(s): _____

      Bequest List Location: _____

7.   Item: _____ Recipient Name(s): _____

      Bequest List Location: _____

8.   Item: _____ Recipient Name(s): _____

      Bequest List Location: _____

BENEFICIARIES & INHERITANCE – 2025 EDITION

Messages or Letters for Beneficiaries:

Location(s): _____

Notes on Disinheritance or Special Instructions:

Details: _____

Document Locations & Keys:

Wills / Bequest Letters: _____

Life Insurance Policies: _____

_____

Employment Agreement: _____

Social Security: _____

Retirement: _____

Veteran's Benefits: _____

Additional Notes:

SECTION 6
PERSONAL PROPERTY & REAL ESTATE

DETAILS MATTER—LISTING YOUR PROPERTIES, DEEDS, AND VALUABLE PERSONAL ITEMS ENSURES NOTHING IS OVERLOOKED AND THAT THE RIGHT PEOPLE RECEIVE WHAT YOU INTENDED.

Scan the QR code
with your phone.

PERSONAL PROPERTY & REAL ESTATE – 2025 EDITION

Primary Residence Details:

Address: _____

Co-Owners: _____

Home Security Company Contact: _____

Mortgage Info & Location of Keys: _____

Additional Properties:

1. Address: _____

   Co-Owners: _____

   Home Security Company Contact: _____

   Mortgage Info & Location of Keys: _____

2. Address: _____

   Co-Owners: _____

   Home Security Company Contact: _____

   Mortgage Info & Location of Keys: _____

3. Address: _____

   Co-Owners: _____

   Home Security Company Contact: _____

   Mortgage Info & Location of Keys: _____

4. Address: _____

   Co-Owners: _____

   Home Security Company Contact: _____

   Mortgage Info & Location of Keys: _____

Deeds & Tax Info Locations:

Stored At: _____

Storage Units & Garages:

1. Location: _____

    Access Details: _____

2. Location: _____

    Access Details: _____

3. Location: _____

    Access Details: _____

High-Value Items & Appraisals:

Item(s): _____

_____

_____

Appraisal Document Location: _____

Photo Albums & Family Keepsakes:

Stored At: _____

Home Contents & Distribution Plan:

Plan Location / Notes: _____

_____

_____

_____

Firearms:

1. Registration Info: _____

   Permit Info: _____

   Legal Documents & Permit Papers: _____

2. Registration Info: _____

   Permit Info: _____

   Legal Documents & Permit Papers: _____

3. Registration Info: _____

   Permit Info: _____

   Legal Documents & Permit Papers: _____

Other Property:

Details: _____

_____

_____

_____

_____

_____

_____

_____

DIGITAL LIFE, SUBSCRIPTIONS, & PASSWORDS

YOUR DIGITAL LIFE IS JUST AS IMPORTANT—MAKE IT EASIER FOR YOUR LOVED ONES TO MANAGE OR CLOSE YOUR ACCOUNTS BY SHARING ACCESS AND INSTRUCTIONS.

Scan the QR code
with your phone.

DIGITAL LIFE, SUBSCRIPTIONS, & PASSWORDS – 2025 EDITION

Password Managers:

Used? ☐ Yes ☐ No

Service Name: _____

Access Info / Master Password: _____

Two-Factor Authentication Devices:

Device(s) Used: _____

Backup Codes Location: _____

Email, Social & Cloud Accounts:

Email Provider(s): _____

Social Media (List Accounts): _____

_____

_____

Cloud Storage (Google Drive, iCloud, etc.): _____

_____

Streaming, Shopping & Productivity Services:

Accounts (Netflix, Amazon, etc.): _____

_____

_____

_____

Cancelation Instructions: _____

_____

_____

DIGITAL LIFE, SUBSCRIPTIONS, & PASSWORDS – 2025 EDITION

Mobile Devices & Laptops:

Type(s): _____

_____

Passcodes / Unlock Info: _____

USBs & External Storage:

Stored At: _____

Instructions for Digital Executor:

Name: _____

Document Location: _____

Email Accounts:

1. Email: _____ Username: _____

   Password: _____ Notes: _____

2. Email: _____ Username: _____

   Password: _____ Notes: _____

3. Email: _____ Username: _____

   Password: _____ Notes: _____

4. Email: _____ Username: _____

   Password: _____ Notes: _____

5.   Email: _____   Username: _____

      Password: _____   Notes: _____

6.   Email: _____   Username: _____

      Password: _____   Notes: _____

7.   Email: _____   Username: _____

      Password: _____   Notes: _____

8.   Email: _____   Username: _____

      Password: _____   Notes: _____

9.   Email: _____   Username: _____

      Password: _____   Notes: _____

10. Email: _____   Username: _____

      Password: _____   Notes: _____

11. Email: _____   Username: _____

      Password: _____   Notes: _____

12. Email: _____   Username: _____

      Password: _____   Notes: _____

DIGITAL LIFE, SUBSCRIPTIONS, & PASSWORDS – 2025 EDITION

Websites:

1.   Website: _____   Username: _____

      Password: _____   Registered Email: _____

2.   Website: _____   Username: _____

      Password: _____   Registered Email: _____

3.   Website: _____   Username: _____

      Password: _____   Registered Email: _____

4.   Website: _____   Username: _____

      Password: _____   Registered Email: _____

5.   Website: _____   Username: _____

      Password: _____   Registered Email: _____

6.   Website: _____   Username: _____

      Password: _____   Registered Email: _____

7.   Website: _____   Username: _____

      Password: _____   Registered Email: _____

8.   Website: _____   Username: _____

      Password: _____   Registered Email: _____

9.   Website: _____   Username: _____

      Password: _____   Registered Email: _____

10.   Website: _____   Username: _____

      Password: _____   Registered Email: _____

11..   Website: _____   Username: _____

      Password: _____   Registered Email: _____

12.   Website: _____   Username: _____

      Password: _____   Registered Email: _____

DIGITAL LIFE, SUBSCRIPTIONS, & PASSWORDS – 2025 EDITION

Blogs:

1. Website / Blog: _____ Username: _____

   Password: _____ Admin Info: _____

   Domain Hosting Service: _____

   Notes: _____

2. Website / Blog: _____ Username: _____

   Password: _____ Admin Info: _____

   Domain Hosting Service: _____

   Notes: _____

3. Website / Blog: _____ Username: _____

   Password: _____ Admin Info: _____

   Domain Hosting Service: _____

   Notes: _____

4. Website / Blog: _____ Username: _____

   Password: _____ Admin Info: _____

   Domain Hosting Service: _____

   Notes: _____

5. Website / Blog: _____ Username: _____

   Password: _____ Admin Info: _____

   Domain Hosting Service: _____

   Notes: _____

   _____

   _____

6. Website / Blog: _____ Username: _____

   Password: _____ Admin Info: _____

   Domain Hosting Service: _____

   Notes: _____

   _____

   _____

7. Website / Blog: _____ Username: _____

   Password: _____ Admin Info: _____

   Domain Hosting Service: _____

   Notes: _____

   _____

   _____

8. Website / Blog: _____ Username: _____

   Password: _____ Admin Info: _____

   Domain Hosting Service: _____

   Notes: _____

   _____

   _____

Additional Notes:

KEY CONTACTS

KEEP YOUR CONTACT LIST UPDATED—OUTDATED INFORMATION CAN CAUSE DELAYS WHEN IT MATTERS MOST.

SkillBinder

Scan the QR code
with your phone.

KEY CONTACTS – 2025 EDITION

Immediate Family Members:

1. Name: _____ Relationship: _____

   Phone: _____ Email: _____

2. Name: _____ Relationship: _____

   Phone: _____ Email: _____

3. Name: _____ Relationship: _____

   Phone: _____ Email: _____

4. Name: _____ Relationship: _____

   Phone: _____ Email: _____

5. Name: _____ Relationship: _____

   Phone: _____ Email: _____

6. Name: _____ Relationship: _____

   Phone: _____ Email: _____

7. Name: _____ Relationship: _____

   Phone: _____ Email: _____

8. Name: _____ Relationship: _____

   Phone: _____ Email: _____

9. Name: _____ Relationship: _____

   Phone: _____ Email: _____

10. Name: _____ Relationship: _____

    Phone: _____ Email: _____

11. Name: _____ Relationship: _____

    Phone: _____ Email: _____

12. Name: _____ Relationship: _____

    Phone: _____ Email: _____

KEY CONTACTS – 2025 EDITION

Friends & Chosen Family:

1. Name: _____ Relationship: _____

   Phone: _____ Email: _____

2. Name: _____ Relationship: _____

   Phone: _____ Email: _____

3. Name: _____ Relationship: _____

   Phone: _____ Email: _____

4. Name: _____ Relationship: _____

   Phone: _____ Email: _____

5. Name: _____ Relationship: _____

   Phone: _____ Email: _____

6. Name: _____ Relationship: _____

   Phone: _____ Email: _____

7. Name: _____ Relationship: _____

   Phone: _____ Email: _____

8. Name: _____ Relationship: _____

   Phone: _____ Email: _____

9. Name: _____ Relationship: _____

   Phone: _____ Email: _____

10. Name: _____ Relationship: _____

    Phone: _____ Email: _____

11. Name: _____ Relationship: _____

    Phone: _____ Email: _____

12. Name: _____ Relationship: _____

    Phone: _____ Email: _____

KEY CONTACTS – 2025 EDITION

Attorney, CPA, Financial Advisor, Tax Preparer, Insurance Agent:

1. Name: _____ Duty: _____

   Phone: _____ Email: _____

2. Name: _____ Duty: _____

   Phone: _____ Email: _____

3. Name: _____ Duty: _____

   Phone: _____ Email: _____

4. Name: _____ Duty: _____

   Phone: _____ Email: _____

Doctor, Caregiver, Healthcare Proxy:

1. Name: _____ Duty: _____

   Phone: _____ Email: _____

2. Name: _____ Duty: _____

   Phone: _____ Email: _____

3. Name: _____ Duty: _____

   Phone: _____ Email: _____

Hairdresser, Handyman, Mechanic, Housekeeper:

1. Name: _____ Duty: _____

   Phone: _____ Email: _____

2. Name: _____ Duty: _____

   Phone: _____ Email: _____

3. Name: _____ Duty: _____

   Phone: _____ Email: _____

4. Name: _____ Duty: _____

   Phone: _____ Email: _____

KEY CONTACTS – 2025 EDITION

Pet Professionals (Vet, Groomer, Sitter Info, etc.):

1. Name: _____   Duty: _____

   Phone: _____   Email: _____

2. Name: _____   Duty: _____

   Phone: _____   Email: _____

Notification List of Who and Who NOT to Contact:

1. ☐ Notify ☐ Do NOT Notify:

   Name: _____   Affiliation to You: _____

   Phone: _____   Email: _____

2. ☐ Notify ☐ Do NOT Notify:

   Name: _____   Affiliation to You: _____

   Phone: _____   Email: _____

3. ☐ Notify ☐ Do NOT Notify:

   Name: _____   Affiliation to You: _____

   Phone: _____   Email: _____

4. ☐ Notify ☐ Do NOT Notify:

   Name: _____   Affiliation to You: _____

   Phone: _____   Email: _____

5. ☐ Notify ☐ Do NOT Notify:

   Name: _____   Affiliation to You: _____

   Phone: _____   Email: _____

6. ☐ Notify ☐ Do NOT Notify:

   Name: _____   Affiliation to You: _____

   Phone: _____   Email: _____

Additional Notes:

SECTION 9
FUNERAL & FINAL ARRANGEMENTS

THE MORE DECISIONS YOU MAKE NOW, THE FEWER YOUR LOVED ONES
WILL NEED TO MAKE DURING GRIEF—OUTLINE YOUR WISHES
FOR A MEANINGFUL FAREWELL.

Scan the QR code
with your phone.

FUNERAL & FINAL ARRANGEMENTS – 2025 EDITION

Burial / Cremation / Donation Wishes:

☐ Burial   ☐ Cremation   ☐ Donation

Details or Restrictions: _____

_____

_____

_____

Preferred Funeral or Memorial Style (Religious, green burial, celebration of life, etc.):

Type: _____

_____

_____

_____

Service Details:

Music: _____

Readings / Rituals: _____

Officiant / Speaker: _____

Guest List or Privacy Preferences:

Public / Private: ☐ Public   ☐ Private

Notes: _____

_____

_____

FUNERAL & FINAL ARRANGEMENTS – 2025 EDITION

Obituary Instructions:

Pre-written? ☐ Yes ☐ No

Stored At: _____

Headstone / Marker Preferences:

☐ Headstone ☐ Plaque ☐ No Marker ☐ Other: _____

Material Preference (e.g., granite, bronze, etc.): _____

Inscription / Epitaph Text: _____

_____

Design Details (symbols, images, layout): _____

Preferred Location or Placement Notes: _____

Responsible Person / Organization: _____

Donations in Lieu of Flowers:

Organization(s): _____

Special Rituals or Tributes:

Details: _____

_____

_____

_____

_____

Additional Notes:

ACCOUNTS & MEMBERSHIPS

SMALL THINGS ADD UP—DOCUMENTING EVERYTHING FROM STORE MEMBERSHIPS TO LOYALTY PROGRAMS AND CLUB ACCOUNTS HELPS LOVED ONES MANAGE CLOSURES, COLLECT BENEFITS, OR CONTINUE WHAT MATTERS.

Scan the QR code
with your phone.

ACCOUNTS & MEMBERSHIPS – 2025 EDITION

Golf Clubs(s):

Details: _____

Social Club(s):

Details: _____

Business Club(s):

Details: _____

Automotive Club(s):

Details: _____

Other Club(s):

Details: _____

Streaming & Subscriptions (Netflix, Hulu, Prime Video, etc):

1. Service Name: _____

    Username: _____ Password: _____

2. Service Name: _____

    Username: _____ Password: _____

3. Service Name: _____

    Username: _____ Password: _____

4.   Service Name: _____

     Username: _____ Password: _____

5.   Service Name: _____

     Username: _____ Password: _____

6.   Service Name: _____

     Username: _____ Password: _____

7.   Service Name: _____

     Username: _____ Password: _____

8.   Service Name: _____

     Username: _____ Password: _____

9.   Service Name: _____

     Username: _____ Password: _____

10. Service Name: _____

     Username: _____ Password: _____

Shopping & Delivery Services (Amazon, Instacart, etc):

1.   Service Name: _____

     Username: _____ Password: _____

2.   Service Name: _____

     Username: _____ Password: _____

3.   Service Name: _____

     Username: _____ Password: _____

4.   Service Name: _____

     Username: _____ Password: _____

ACCOUNTS & MEMBERSHIPS – 2025 EDITION

Financial Apps & Wallets (PayPal, Venmo, etc):

1.   Service Name: _____

     Username: _____ Password: _____

2.   Service Name: _____

     Username: _____ Password: _____

3.   Service Name: _____

     Username: _____ Password: _____

Publications & Memberships (Magazines, Journals, etc):

1.   Service Name: _____

     Username: _____ Password: _____

2.   Service Name: _____

     Username: _____ Password: _____

3.   Service Name: _____

     Username: _____ Password: _____

Rewards & Points Programs (Credit Card, Retail Rewards, etc):

1.   Service Name: _____

     Username: _____ Password: _____

2.   Service Name: _____

     Username: _____ Password: _____

3.   Service Name: _____

     Username: _____ Password: _____

ACCOUNTS & MEMBERSHIPS – 2025 EDITION

Frequent Flyer Accounts (Airlines, Miles Programs, etc):

1. Service Name: _____

   Username: _____ Password: _____

2. Service Name: _____

   Username: _____ Password: _____

3. Service Name: _____

   Username: _____ Password: _____

Phone, Internet, Utilities:

1. Service Name: _____

   Username: _____ Password: _____

2. Service Name: _____

   Username: _____ Password: _____

3. Service Name: _____

   Username: _____ Password: _____

Store & Travel Loyalty Programs:

Cards / Programs: _____

_____

Miscellaneous:

Details: _____

_____

_____

_____

Additional Notes:

PETS & ANIMAL CARE

PETS ARE FAMILY—INCLUDE ROUTINES, VET INFO, AND FUTURE CAREGIVERS TO ENSURE THEY CONTINUE RECEIVING THE LOVE AND CARE THEY DESERVE.

Scan the QR code
with your phone.

PETS & ANIMAL CARE – 2025 EDITION

Pet Information:

1. Name: _____ Chipped?: ☐Yes ☐No

   Species/Breed: _____

   Age: _____ Diet Needs: _____ Feeding Times: _____

   Medical Needs: _____

   Notes: _____

2. Name: _____ Chipped?: ☐Yes ☐No

   Species/Breed: _____

   Age: _____ Diet Needs: _____ Feeding Times: _____

   Medical Needs: _____

   Notes: _____

3. Name: _____ Chipped?: ☐Yes ☐No

   Species/Breed: _____

   Age: _____ Diet Needs: _____ Feeding Times: _____

   Medical Needs: _____

   Notes: _____

4. Name: _____ Chipped?: ☐Yes ☐No

   Species/Breed: _____

   Age: _____ Diet Needs: _____ Feeding Times: _____

   Medical Needs: _____

   Notes: _____

5. Name: _____ Chipped?: ☐Yes ☐No

   Species/Breed: _____

   Age: _____ Diet Needs: _____ Feeding Times: _____

   Medical Needs: _____

   Notes: _____

PETS & ANIMAL CARE – 2025 EDITION

Veterinarian Information:

1.   Clinic Name: _____   Phone: _____

1.   Clinic Name: _____   Phone: _____

1.   Clinic Name: _____   Phone: _____

Pet Insurance:

Insurance Provider: _____

Policy Number: _____   Contact Info: _____

Primary & Backup Caregivers:

Primary Caregiver Name: _____   Contact Info: _____

Backup Caregiver Name: _____   Contact Info: _____

Supplies & Comfort Items:

Important Items (bed, toy, blanket): _____

Item Locations: _____

Legacy Wishes for Pets:

☐ Keep in Family   ☐ Rehome   ☐ Shelter Placement

Additional Notes: _____

Instructions for Foster or Rehoming:

Preferred Organization or Person: _____

Contact Info & Notes: _____

Additional Notes:

SHORT LETTERS TO LOVED ONES

YOUR WORDS WILL LAST FOREVER—USE THIS SPACE TO LEAVE MEANINGFUL
MESSAGES, REFLECTIONS, OR BLESSINGS TO THOSE WHO MATTER MOST.

Scan the QR code
with your phone.

Recipient Names & Relationships:

Name: _____ Releationship: _____

Letter: _____

_____

_____

_____

_____

_____

_____

_____

_____

_____

_____

_____

_____

_____

_____

SHORT LETTERS TO LOVED ONES – 2025 EDITION

Name: _____ Releationship: _____

Letter: _____

SHORT LETTERS TO LOVED ONES – 2025 EDITION

Name: _____ Releationship: _____

Letter: _____

SHORT LETTERS TO LOVED ONES – 2025 EDITION

Name: _____ Releationship: _____

Letter: _____

SHORT LETTERS TO LOVED ONES – 2025 EDITION

Name: _____ Releationship: _____

Letter: _____

SHORT LETTERS TO LOVED ONES – 2025 EDITION

Name: _____ Releationship: _____

Letter: _____

_____

_____

_____

_____

_____

_____

_____

_____

_____

_____

_____

_____

_____

_____

_____

_____

_____

_____

_____

SHORT LETTERS TO LOVED ONES – 2025 EDITION

Name: _____ Releationship: _____

Letter: _____

Name: _____ Releationship: _____

Letter: _____

SHORT LETTERS TO LOVED ONES – 2025 EDITION

Name: _____ Releationship: _____

Letter: _____

_____

_____

_____

_____

_____

_____

_____

_____

_____

_____

_____

_____

_____

_____

_____

_____

_____

SHORT LETTERS TO LOVED ONES – 2025 EDITION

Name: _____ Releationship: _____

Letter: _____

SHORT LETTERS TO LOVED ONES – 2025 EDITION

Location of Letters or Recordings:

Stored At: _____

Timing or Delivery Instructions:

☐ At Time of Passing

☐ On Specific Date/Event

Instructions for Delivery: _____

Video or Audio Messages:

1. Recipient: ☐ Individual or ☐ Group   Message Recorded? ☐ Yes ☐ No

   Name of Individual or Group: _____

   Location of Recording: _____

2. Recipient: ☐ Individual or ☐ Group   Message Recorded? ☐ Yes ☐ No

   Name of Individual or Group: _____

   Location of Recording: _____

3. Recipient: ☐ Individual or ☐ Group   Message Recorded? ☐ Yes ☐ No

   Name of Individual or Group: _____

   Location of Recording: _____

4. Recipient: ☐ Individual or ☐ Group   Message Recorded? ☐ Yes ☐ No

   Name of Individual or Group: _____

   Location of Recording: _____

5. Recipient: ☐ Individual or ☐ Group   Message Recorded? ☐ Yes ☐ No

   Name of Individual or Group: _____

   Location of Recording: _____

SHORT LETTERS TO LOVED ONES – 2025 EDITION

Final Reflections or Blessings:

Personal Notes: _____

_____

_____

_____

_____

_____

_____

_____

_____

Spiritual or Cultural Messages: _____

_____

_____

_____

_____

_____

_____

_____

_____

Additional Notes:

SECTION 13
FINAL WISHES & LEGACY PLANNING

YOUR VALUES LIVE ON—SHARE YOUR LIFE LESSONS, TRADITIONS, AND HOPES FOR THE FUTURE TO LEAVE BEHIND MORE THAN JUST INSTRUCTIONS.

Scan the QR code
with your phone.

FINAL WISHES & LEGACY PLANNING – 2025 EDITION

Ethical Will or Values Statement:

☐ Written ☐ Video

Location: _____

Creative or Personal Legacy Projects:

Description: _____

_____

Stored or Shared Where: _____

Charitable Donations or Scholarships:

Organization / Cause: _____

_____

_____

_____

_____

Donation Instructions or Funds Set Aside: _____

_____

_____

_____

_____

Life Lessons, Sayings, and Humor:

Favorite Sayings / Advice: _____

_____

_____

_____

_____

Personal Stories or Traditions to Share: _____

_____

_____

_____

_____

_____

Instructions for Family Traditions, Archives, Recipes:

Details or Items to Preserve: _____

_____

_____

_____

_____

Location: _____

_____

FINAL WISHES & LEGACY PLANNING – 2025 EDITION

Wishes for How to Be Remembered:

Personal Legacy Statement: _____

_____

_____

_____

_____

_____

_____

Preferred Tributes or Memorials: _____

_____

_____

_____

_____

_____

_____

_____

BUCKET LIST & UNFINISHED BUSINESS

IT'S NEVER TOO LATE TO DREAM—USE THIS SECTION TO REFLECT ON WHAT
\YOU STILL HOPE TO DO, AND WHAT YOU'D LIKE OTHERS TO KNOW
OR FINISH ON YOUR BEHALF.

Scan the QR code
with your phone.

BUCKET LIST & UNFINISHED BUSINESS – 2025 EDITION

Places to Visit:

1. _____
2. _____
3. _____
4. _____
5. _____
6. _____
7. _____
8. _____
9. _____
10. _____
11. _____
12. _____
13. _____
14. _____
15. _____
16. _____
17. _____
18. _____
19. _____
20. _____

BUCKET LIST & UNFINISHED BUSINESS – 2025 EDITION

Projects to Complete:

1. _____
2. _____
3. _____
4. _____
5. _____
6. _____
7. _____
8. _____
9. _____
10. _____

Messages Left Unsaid:

To Whom: _____

Message Summary and/or Location: _____

_____

_____

_____

_____

_____

_____

_____

BUCKET LIST & UNFINISHED BUSINESS – 2025 EDITION

To Whom: _____

    Message Summary and/or Location: _____

_____

_____

_____

_____

_____

_____

To Whom: _____

    Message Summary and/or Location: _____

_____

_____

_____

_____

_____

_____

BUCKET LIST & UNFINISHED BUSINESS – 2025 EDITION

To Whom:

    Message Summary and/or Location:

To Whom:

    Message Summary and/or Location:

BUCKET LIST & UNFINISHED BUSINESS – 2025 EDITION

Hopes for Family's Future:

1.   Letters or Notes Left: ☐ Yes ☐ No

    What You'd Like for Them to Remember or Pursue: _____

_____

_____

2.   Letters or Notes Left: ☐ Yes ☐ No

    What You'd Like for Them to Remember or Pursue: _____

_____

_____

3.   Letters or Notes Left: ☐ Yes ☐ No

    What You'd Like for Them to Remember or Pursue: _____

_____

_____

4.   Letters or Notes Left: ☐ Yes ☐ No

    What You'd Like for Them to Remember or Pursue: _____

_____

_____

5.   Letters or Notes Left: ☐ Yes ☐ No

    What You'd Like for Them to Remember or Pursue: _____

_____

_____

Time-Sensitive Events or Instructions:

Event / Instruction: _____

Date / Trigger: _____

Closing Thoughts or Farewell Letter:

Letter Written? ☐ Yes ☐ No

Location of Letter: _____

Additional Reflections: _____

_____

_____

_____

_____

_____

_____

_____

_____

_____

_____

_____

_____

_____

Additional Notes:

FORMAL LETTERS – 2025 EDITION

SPEAK FROM THE HEART—THIS IS YOUR CHANCE TO SHARE LOVE, GRATITUDE, MEMORIES, OR FORGIVENESS WITH THE PEOPLE WHO MEANT THE MOST TO YOU.

Scan the QR code
with your phone.

1/4 inch

1/4 inch

1/4 inch

1/4 inch

1/4 inch

1/4 inch

1/4 inch

1/4 inch

1/4 inch

1/4 inch

1/4 inch

CONCLUSION

THANK YOU & GOODBYE

Scan the QR code
with your phone.